Abongi's journey

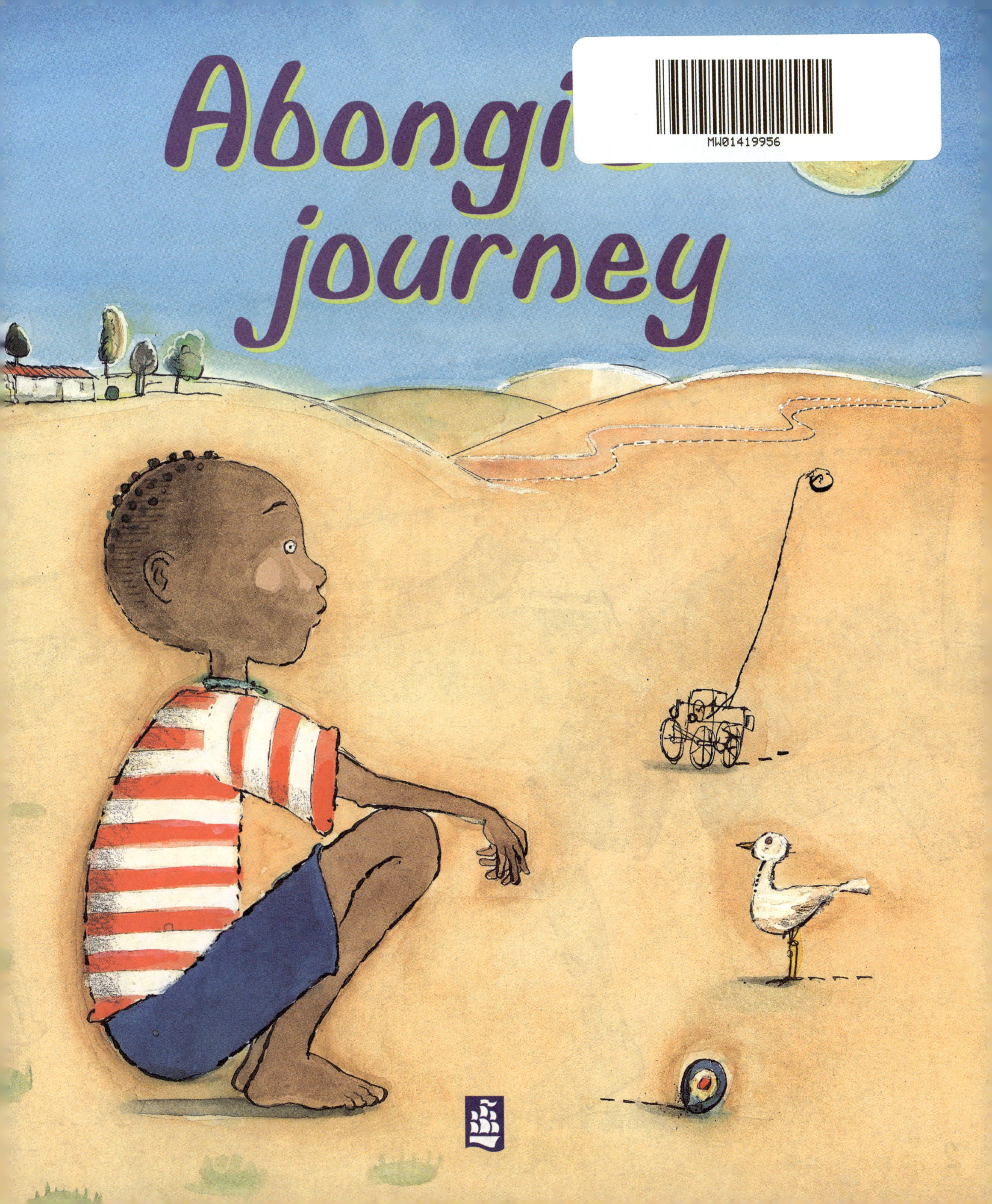

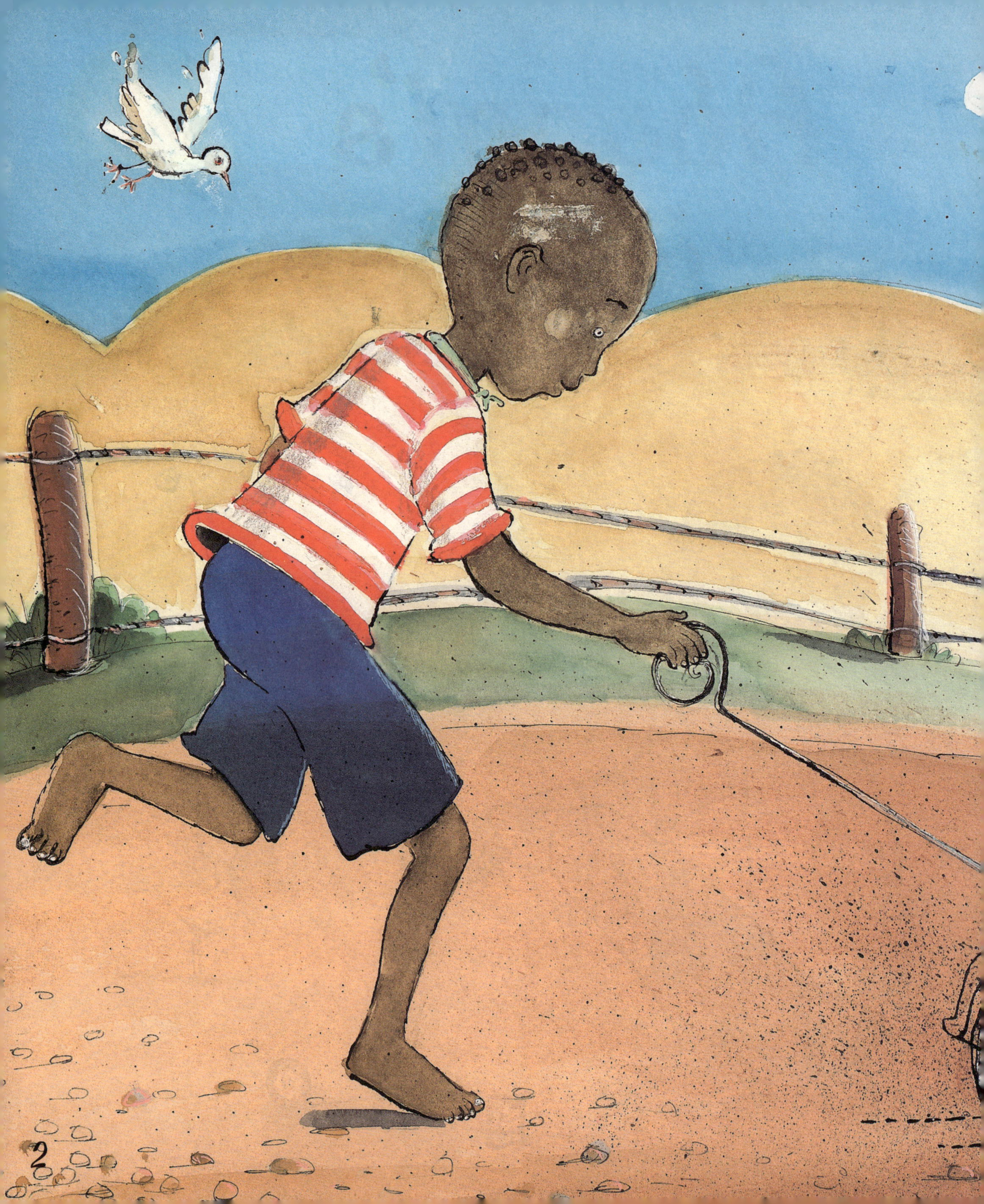

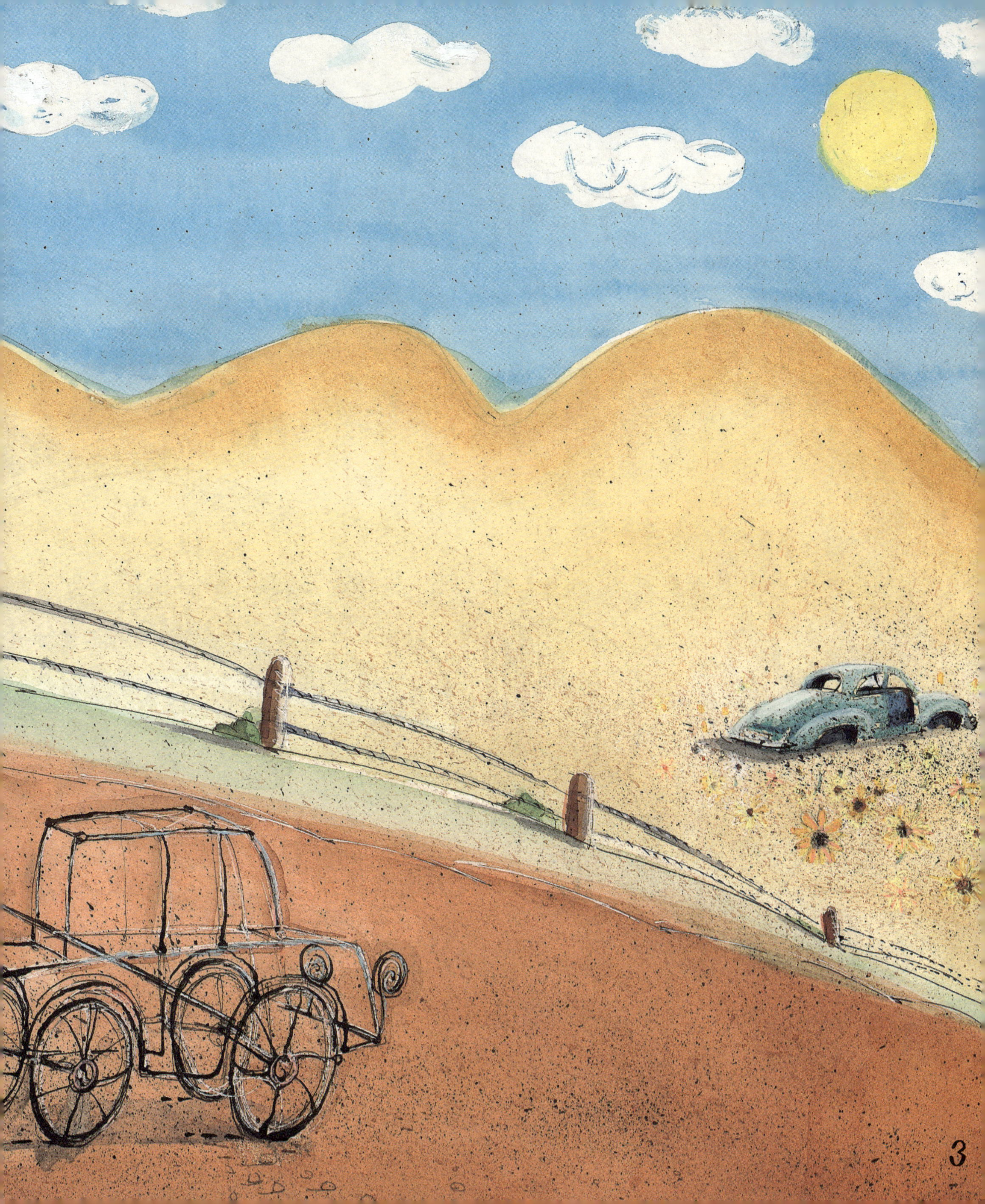

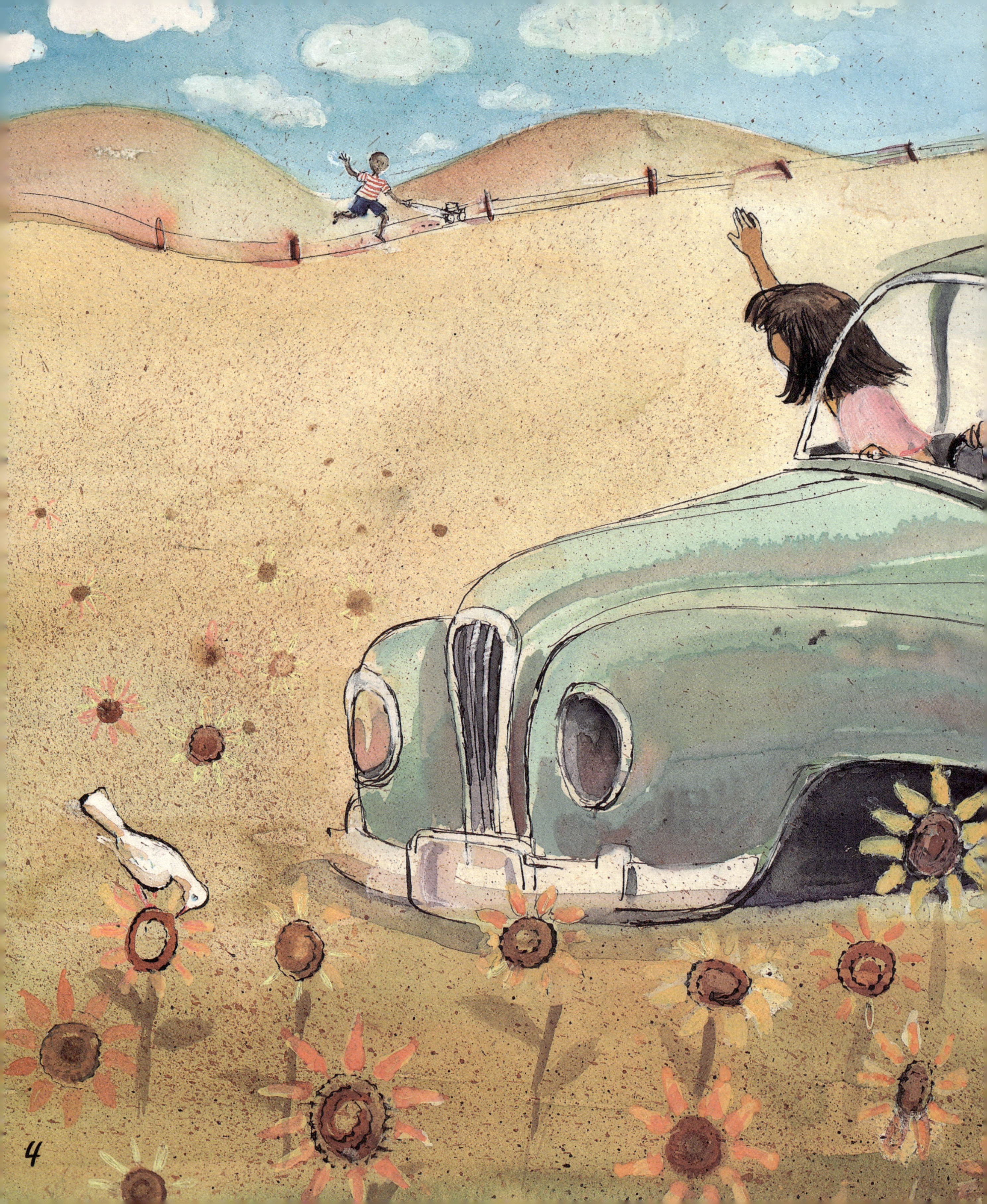

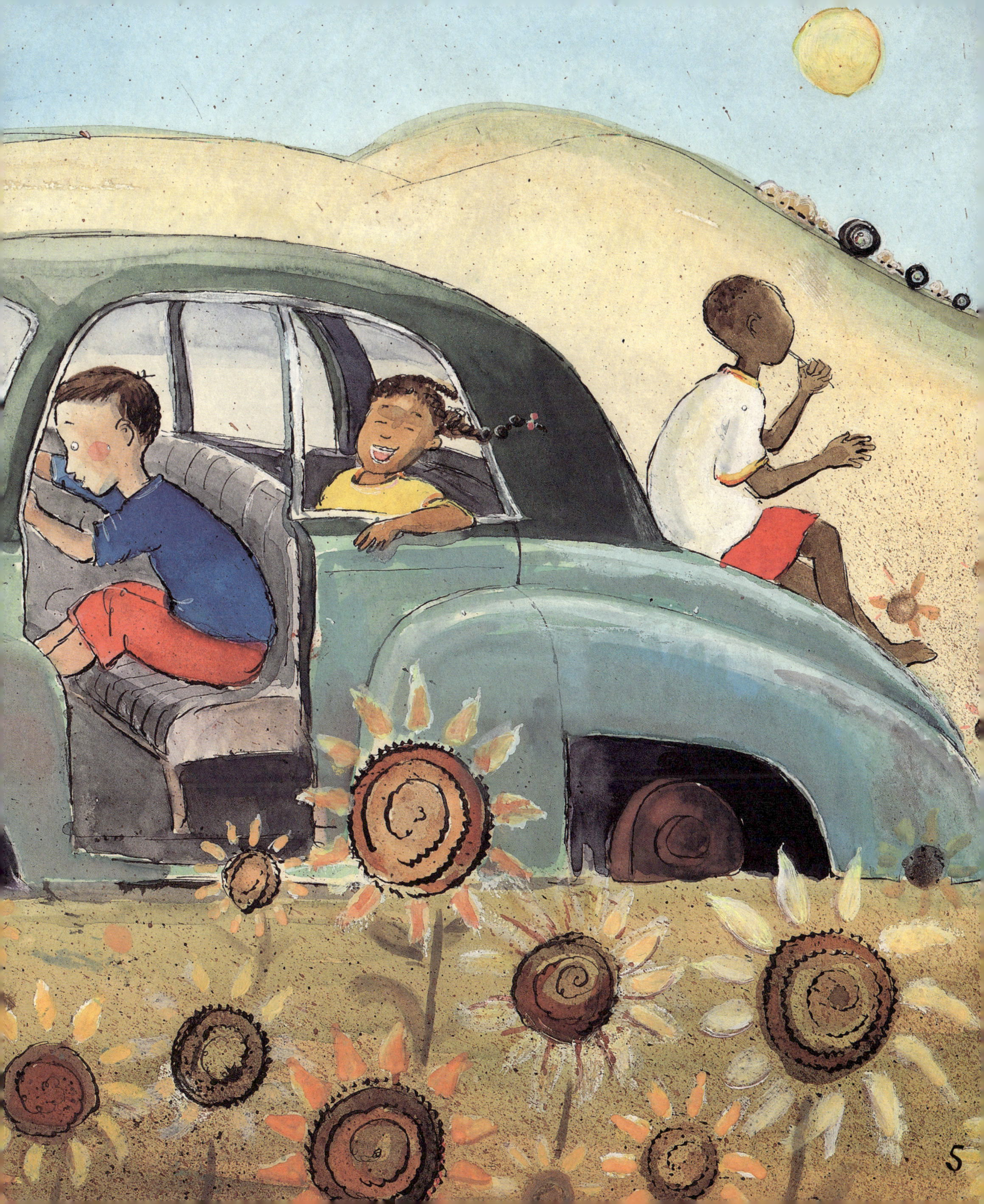

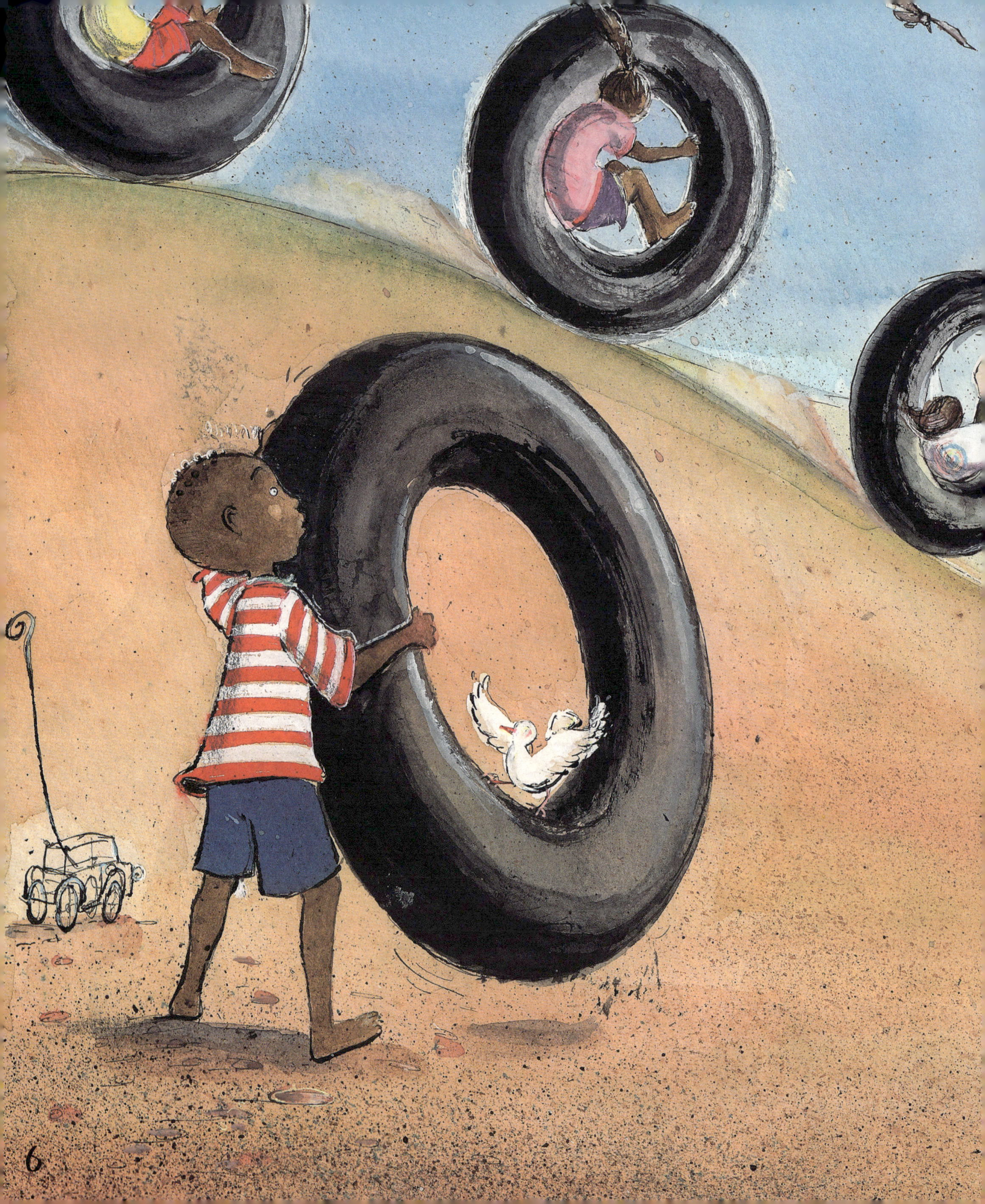

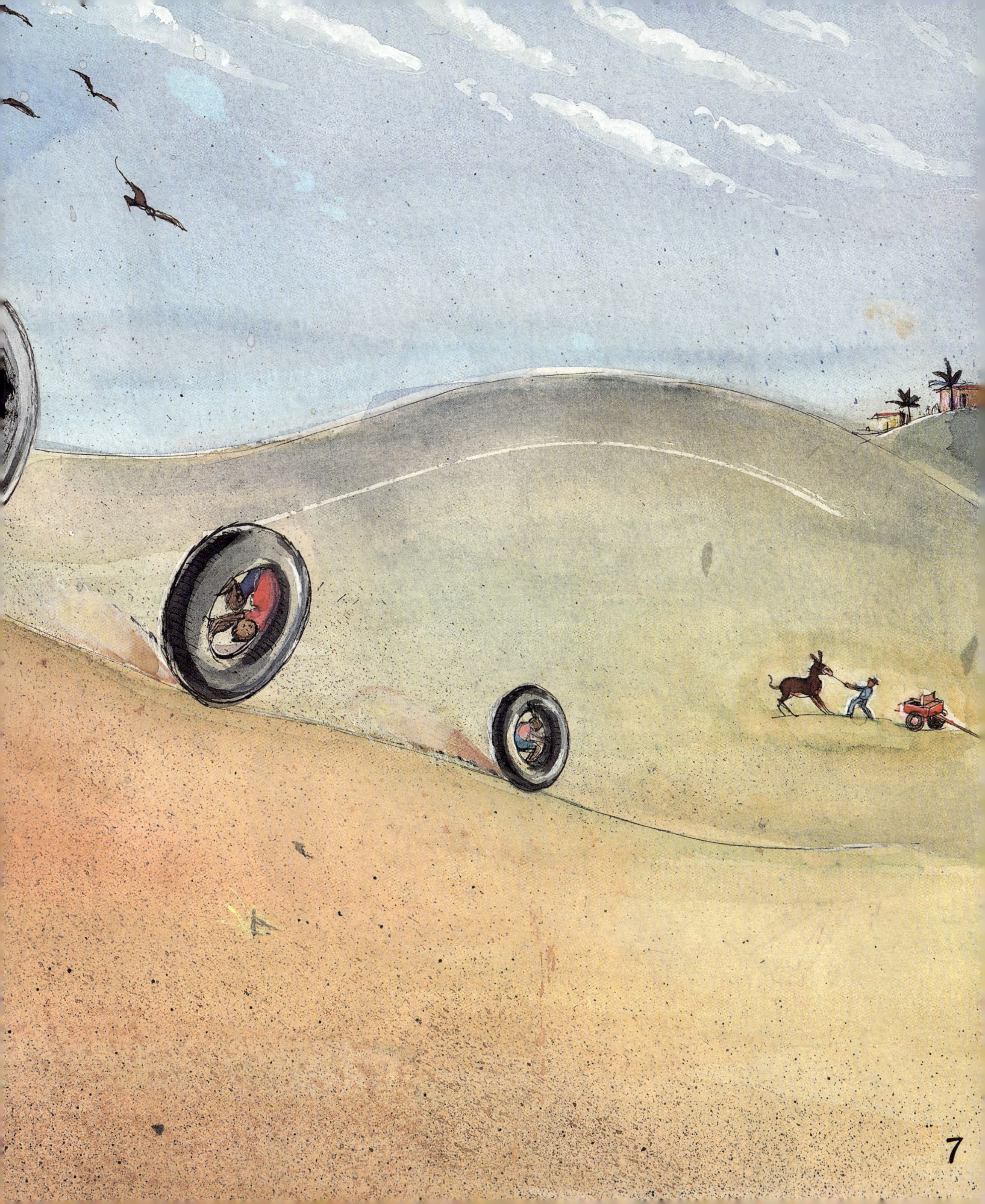

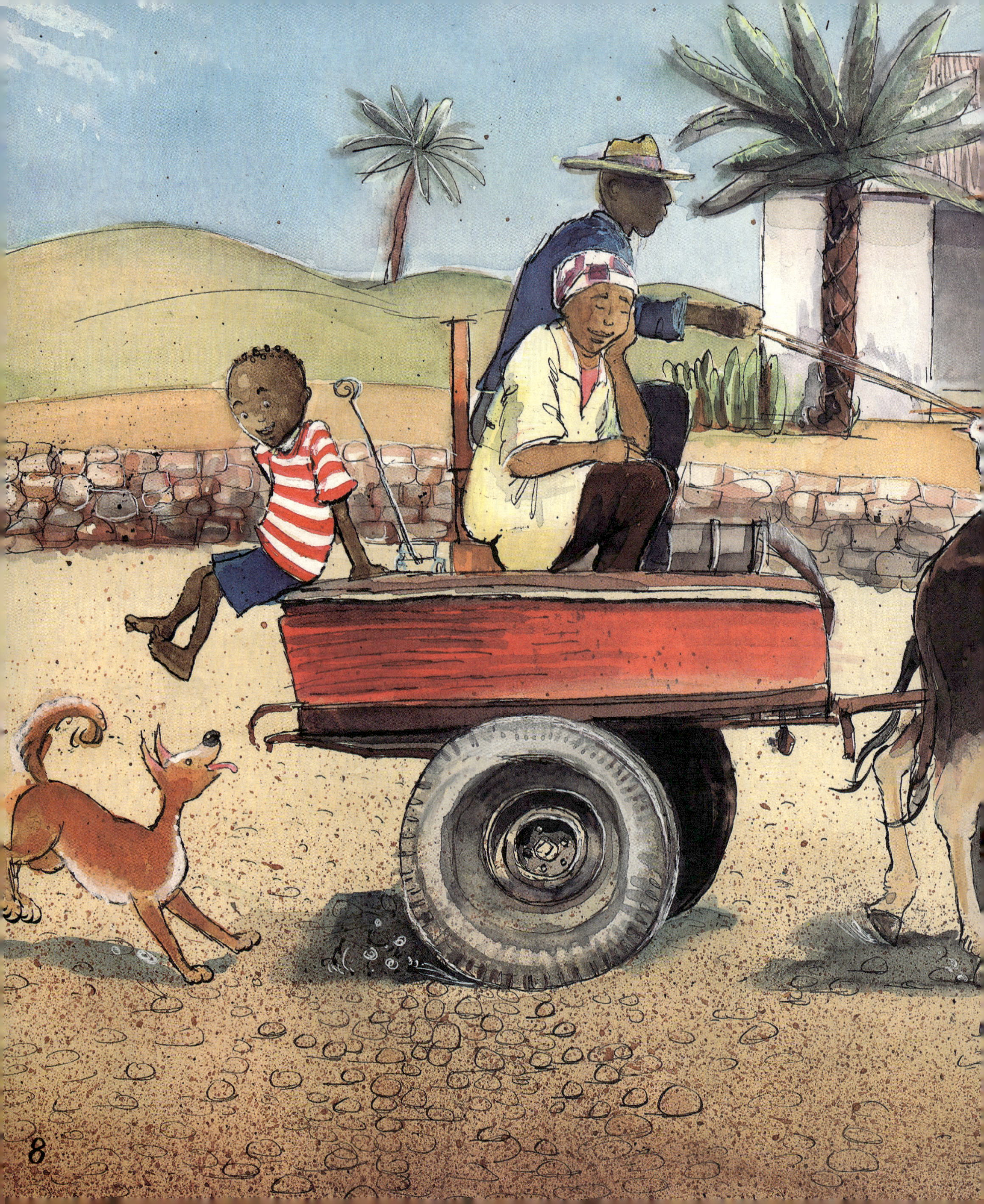

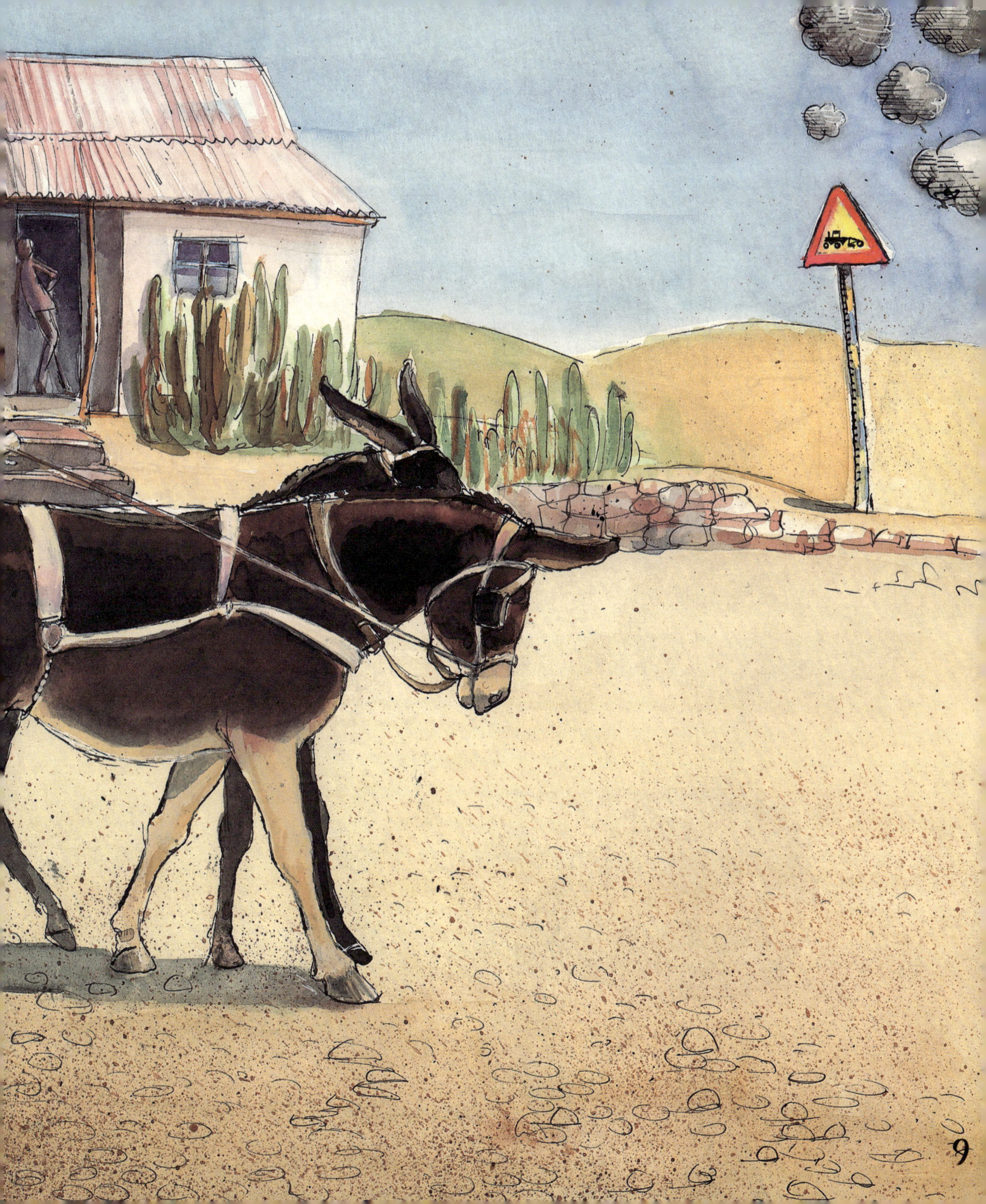

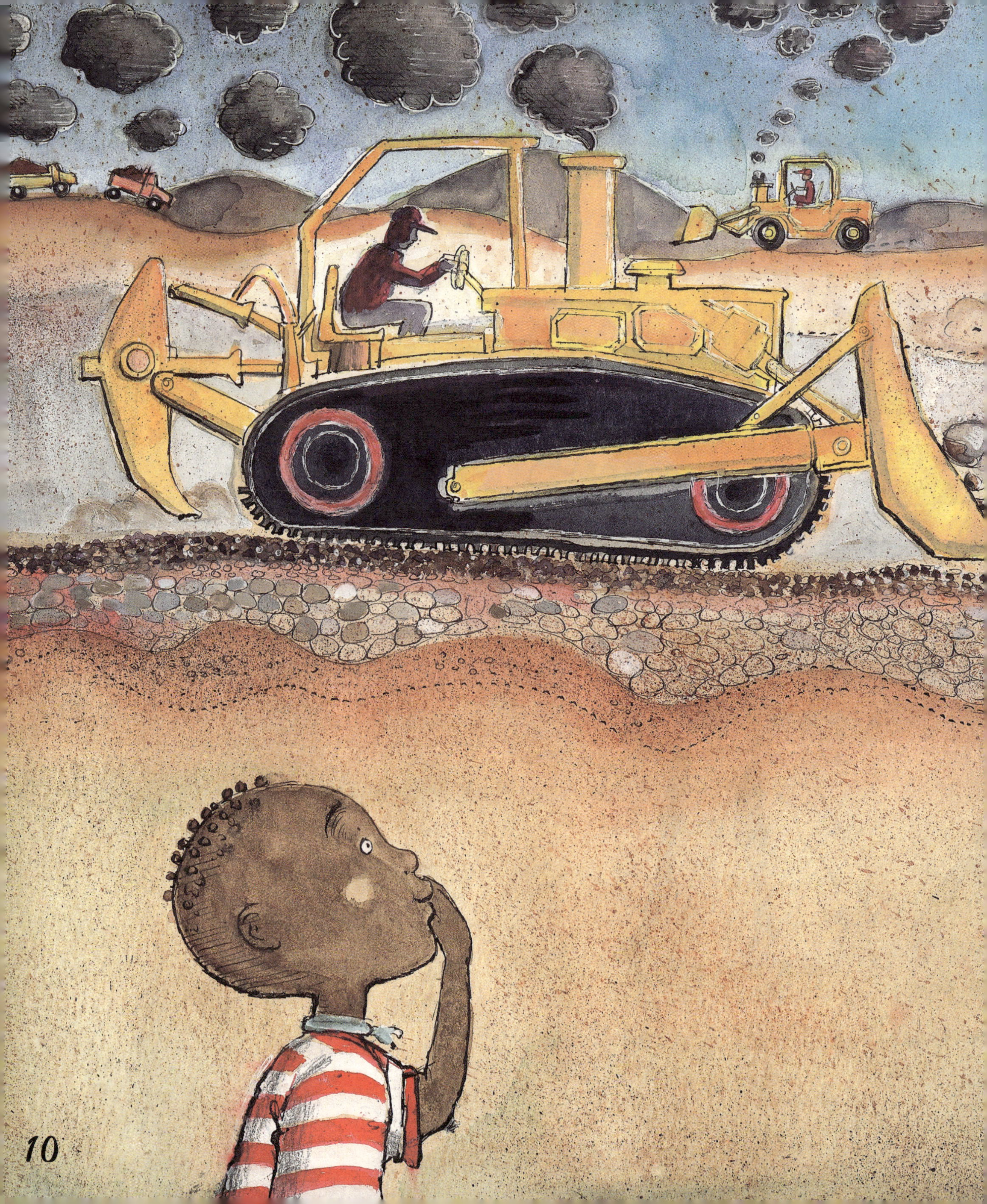

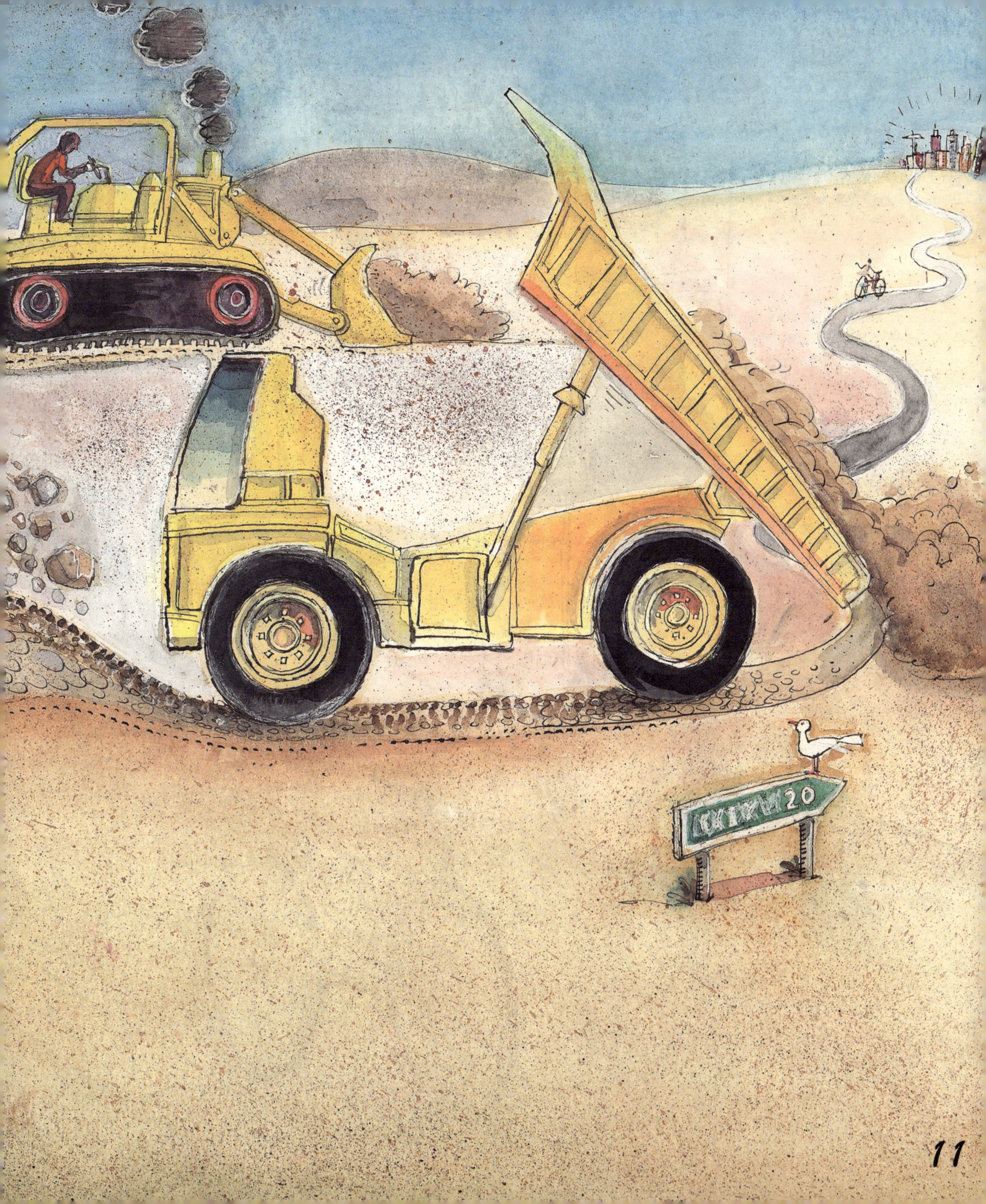
20

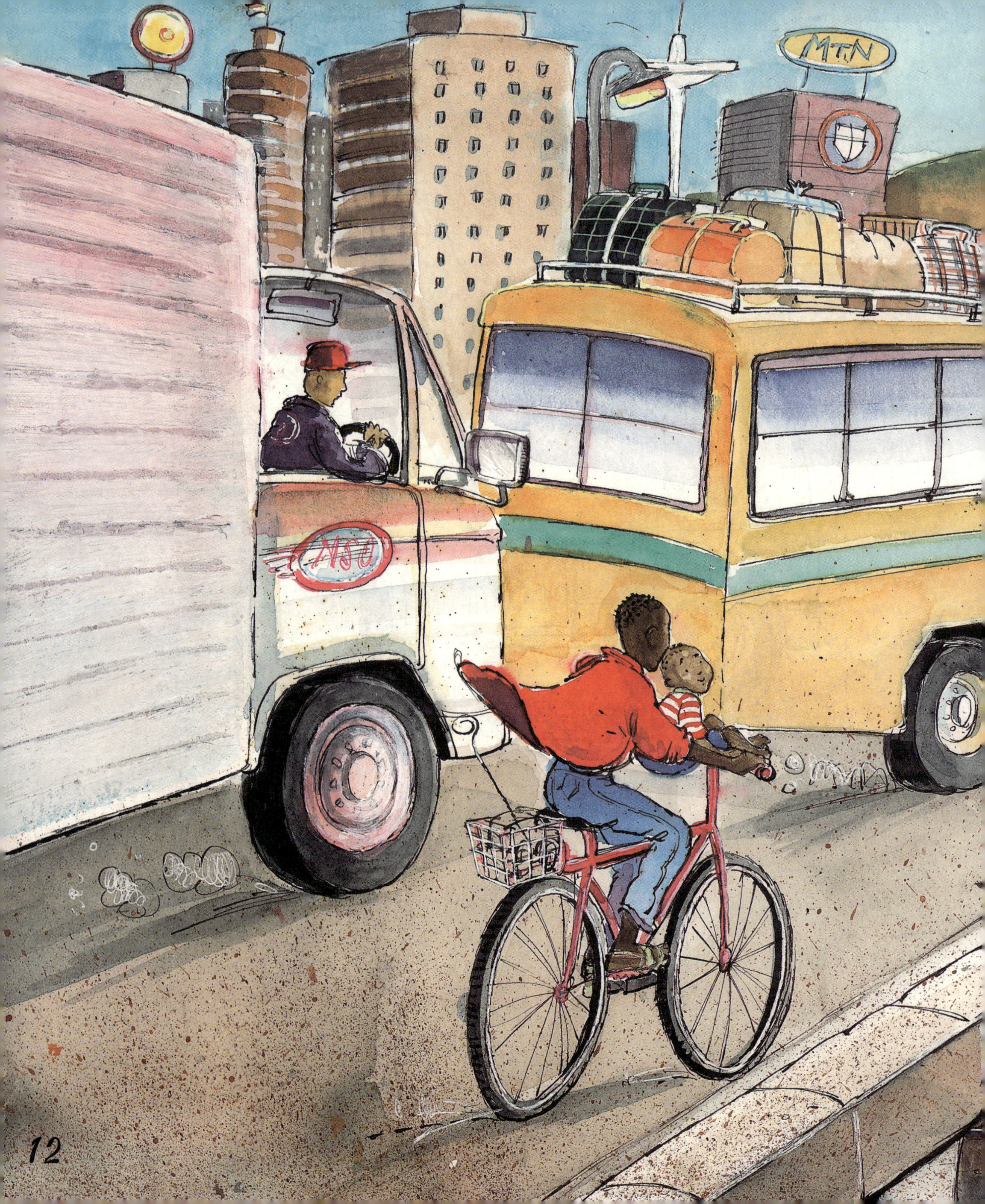
MTN
NSU

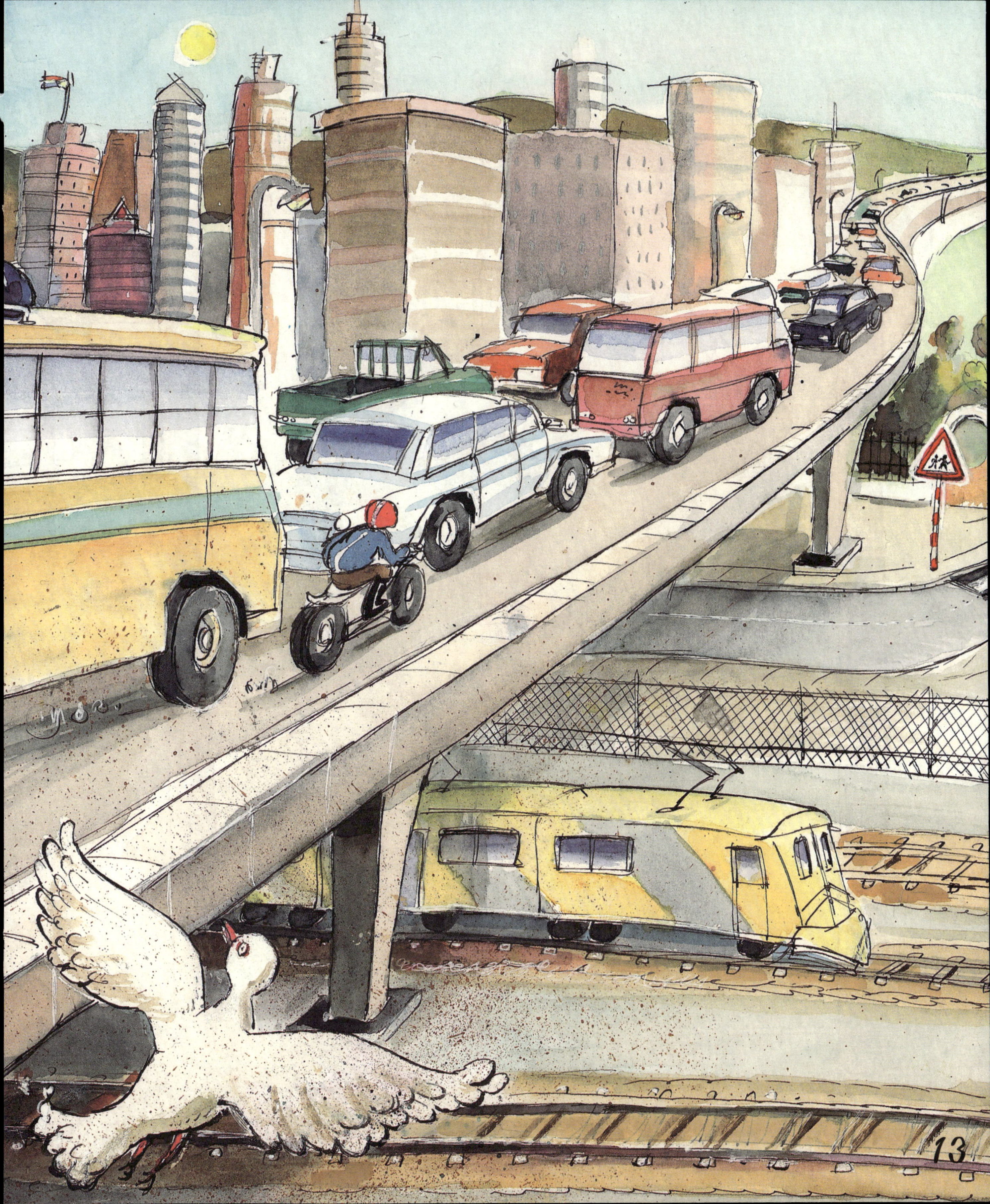

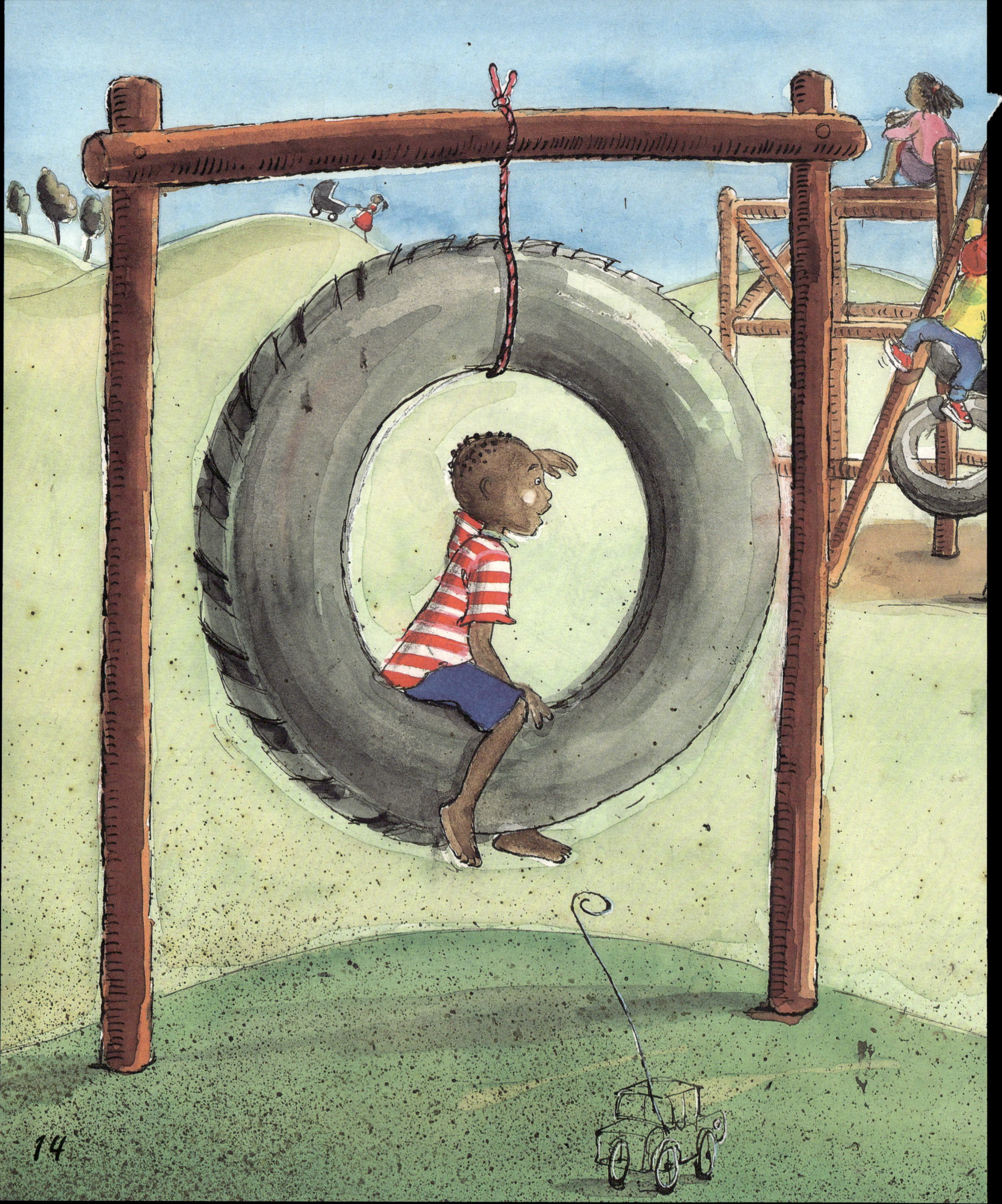

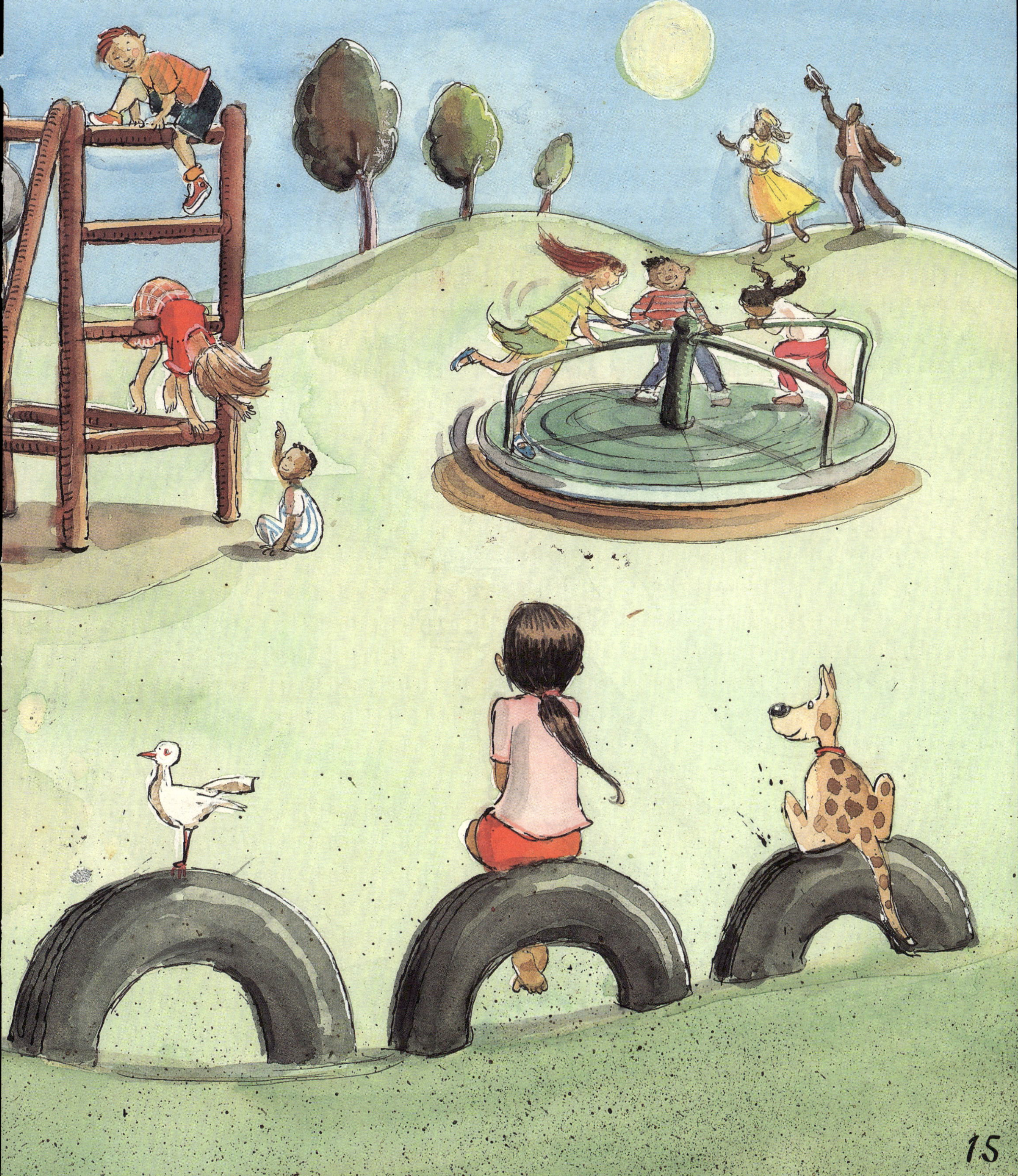

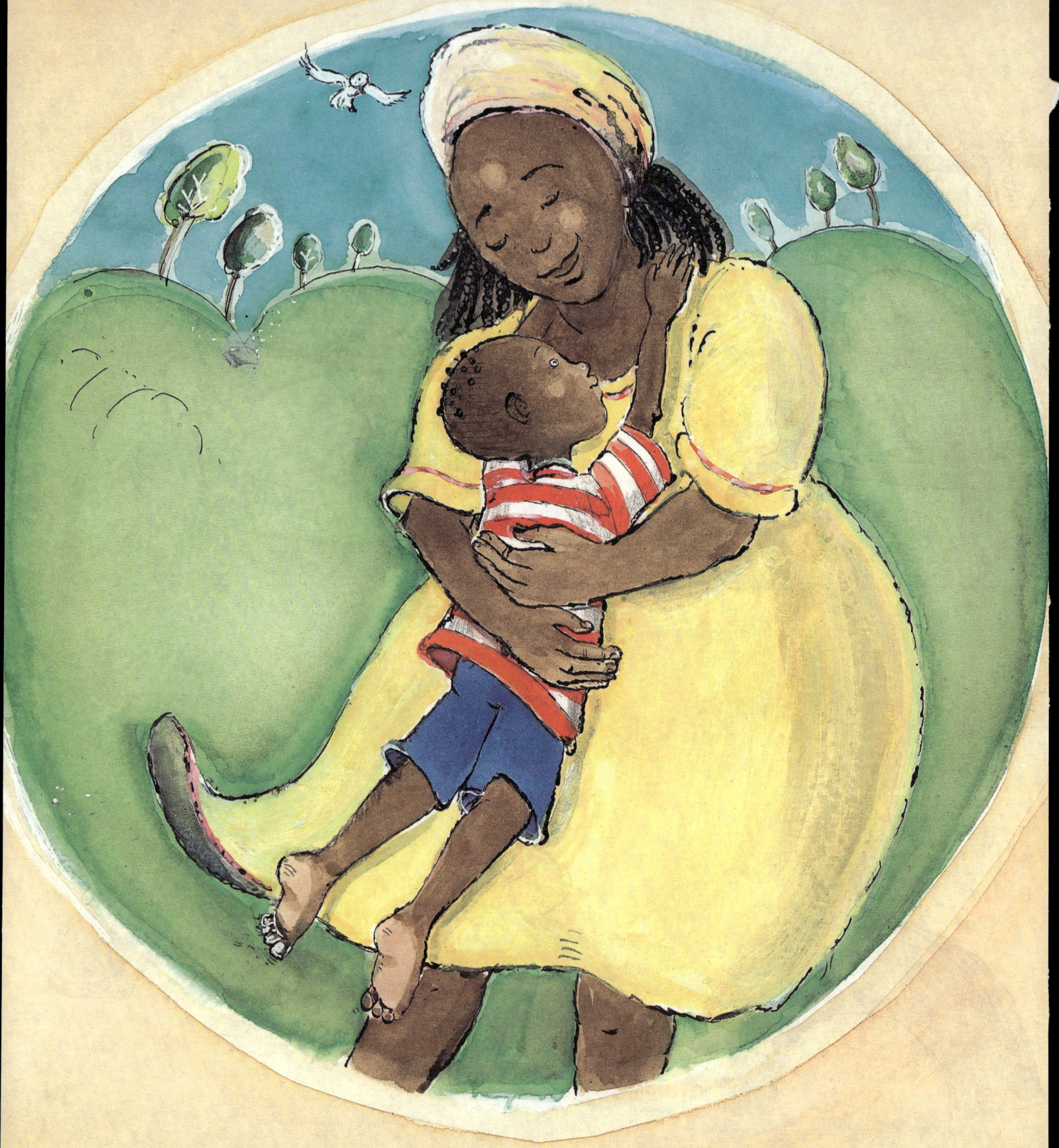